Steve

by Ethan Decker
illustrated by Karen Ortiz

Decodable 19

McGraw Hill Education

Bothell, WA • Chicago, IL • Columbus, OH • New York, NY

MHEonline.com

Send all inquiries to:
McGraw-Hill Education
8787 Orion Place
Columbus, OH 43240

ISBN: 978-0-02-138079-4
MHID: 0-02-138079-1

Printed in China

9 10 11 12 13 DSS 28 27 26 25 24

Yes, Steve is here.

We see him.

But did she see Steve yet?

She has Steves!

She has nine!

She has big Steves and slim Steves.

But there is no Ben.
Just Steves!

There is no Ken.
Just Steves!

She has ten Steves!